Just the Facts

Chemical and Biological Warfare

Adam Hibbert

www.heinemann.co.uk/library
Visit our website to find out more information about **Heinemann Library** books.

To order:
☎ Phone 44 (0) 1865 888066
🖹 Send a fax to 44 (0) 1865 314091
💻 Visit the Heinemann Bookshop at www.heinemann.co.uk/library to browse our catalogue and order online.

Produced by Monkey Puzzle Media Ltd
Gissing's Farm, Fressingfield, Suffolk IP21 5SH, UK

First published in Great Britain by Heinemann Library, Halley Court, Jordan Hill, Oxford OX2 8EJ, part of Harcourt Education.
Heinemann is a registered trademark of Harcourt Education Ltd.

Editorial: Sarah Eason and Georga Godwin
Design: Mark Whitchurch
Picture Research: Sally Cole
Consultant: Simon M. Whitby
Production: Edward Moore

Originated by Dot Gradations Ltd
Printed and bound in Hong Kong, China by
  South China Printing Company

ISBN 0 431 16160 7
07 06 05 04 03
10 9 8 7 6 5 4 3 2 1

British Library Cataloguing in Publication Data
Hibbert, Adam
Chemical and Biological Warfare
358.3
A full catalogue record for this book is available from the British Library.

Acknowledgements
The publishers would like to thank the following for permission to reproduce photographs:
AKG London pp. **5** (Bodleian Library), **13** (British Library), **17**; Associated Press pp. **18–19**, **25** (Alexei Sazonov); Alamy pp. **48** (ImageState), **51** (Nick Cobbing/David Hoffman Photo Library); Corbis pp. **8** (Paul Almasy), **10–11** (Bettmann), **12** (Sally Morgan/ Ecoscene), **20–21** (Ed Kashi), **26–27** (Ron Sanford), **28** (Bolivar Arellano/NY Post/Sygma) **47** (Houston Scott/Sygma); Hulton Archive pp. **15**, **31**; Popperfoto pp. **16**, **24** (Reuters), **29** (Reuters), **35**, **41** (Mike Hutchings/ Reuters); Press Association pp. **4** (EPA), **34** (EPA), **36** (EPA), **43** (EPA), **44** (Canadian Press), **46**; Reuters p. **40** (Toshiyuri Aizawa); Science Photo Library pp. **9** (Richard S. Green), **32** (Cristina Pedrazzini), **33** (Jean-Loup Charmet); Topham Picturepoint pp. **6** (Josh Reynolds/ImageWorks), **23** (ImageWorks), **39** (ImageWorks).

Cover photograph reproduced with permission of Digital Vision.

Every effort has been made to contact copyright holders of any material reproduced in this book. Any omissions will be rectified in subsequent printings if notice is given to the publishers.

Any words appearing in the text in bold, **like this**, are explained in the Glossary.

Contents

Introduction

Today's battles are fought with very different weapons from the ones used in the past. Here, rioters and police wear masks to protect themselves from tear gas – a type of chemical weapon.

Most weapons, from bows and arrows to machine guns, work by causing a direct injury to an enemy's body. Swords, arrows and bullets all pierce the skin, causing bleeding or damaging a vital body part. But chemical and biological weapons are different. Instead of inflicting simple, direct injuries, they cause chemical reactions or diseases that attack the body. In most cases, they harm every person in an area, not just enemy soldiers.

Chemical weapons are created by mixing chemicals together to make poisonous solids, gases or liquids that react with parts of the body, causing severe pain and often death. Biological weapons (or **bioweapons**) are made using the germs that cause disease in humans, animals or plants. These germs can also be bred to create 'super-bugs', which may disable or kill anyone infected with them. Although these two **agents** are made in very different ways, they create very similar problems for society.

Controlling the weapons

Over the last 100 years, international organizations, such as the United Nations (**UN**), have laid down rules for war. These rules are made to try to stop wars causing too much damage. The UN rules (see page 35) state that chemical and biological weapons are totally prohibited unless their use is for peaceful, protective purposes. Certain chemical agents can be used to control riots and enforce law and order, but not in a war situation. However, these rules do not work with people such as **terrorists**, who deliberately break the law and use violence to draw attention to their cause.

Chemical and biological weapons (**CBW**s) are often called Weapons of Mass Destruction (or WMDs) because they cause widespread harm, killing many innocent people as well as enemy soldiers. However, WMDs also include **nuclear weapons**. CBW warfare is different from nuclear warfare, because it can be used by small groups or individuals. Nuclear technology is difficult and expensive, which limits its use to just a few of the most developed countries, but CBWs can be used in **guerrilla** warfare or in terrorist campaigns.

This medieval painting shows knights fighting with swords. Until very recently, people have mainly used weapons that caused direct physical damage to an enemy soldier's body.

Types of weapon

Chemical weapons are usually produced by scientists, who mix different chemicals together in a laboratory to produce poisonous solids, liquids or gases. Biological weapons are harder to make than chemical weapons. Scientists cannot yet build a new **organism** (a living thing, such as a germ), so they have to find one that is already deadly, and then find ways to make it more powerful.

Biological weapons

An effective **bioweapon** has to be able to infect its human targets easily, to reproduce quickly, to spread between targets and to kill or disable people who are infected.

At the same time, it should not be too good at these tasks, or it might get out of control and destroy the users as well as the victims. For this reason, most bioweapons developed by countries have been highly infectious (easy to catch), but not highly contagious – which means they do not spread very easily between people. Anthrax is a good example of a biological weapon that is very infectious but not very contagious.

Chemical weapons

There are at least four types of chemical weapon. The first type is fairly simple. It consists of chemical **agents**, such as pepper spray and CS gas (a gas that smells like pepper, but is even more irritating). These chemicals make their human targets helpless for a short time. They irritate the eyes – which is why they are sometimes known as 'tear gases' – and cause people to have trouble breathing, but their effects wear off quite quickly.

A masked protestor hurls back a canister of tear gas at a line of police.

The second type of chemical is more dangerous. These are substances, such as **mustard gas**, that 'burn' the skin, causing painful blisters and blindness. They are designed to slow an enemy army down, by wounding thousands of soldiers. However, although the damage from these chemicals is long-lasting, they only kill about one per cent of their targets.

The third type of chemical weapon is made from lung-damaging chemicals that can be deadly when they are breathed in. When people breathe in these chemicals, the linings of their lungs produce fluid to protect themselves, and if the lungs fill with fluid, the victim dies. Chlorine gas, which was used in World War I, is an example of a lung-damaging chemical.

The fourth type of chemical weapon is the most complex and the most dangerous. **Nerve agents** penetrate the skin and lung linings, destroying nerves and causing victims to lose control of their bodies. In most cases, nerve agents can cause enough damage to stop the heart beating. An example of a nerve agent is tabun, which was used in the Iran-Iraq War of 1980–88.

Bioweapons

There are two main types of **bioweapon** – **viruses** and **bacteria**. Viruses are the simplest forms of life – tiny particles that need to steal from more complex life forms in order to grow and reproduce. They take over **cells** in a plant or an animal, making millions of copies of themselves. Bacteria are very simple, single-celled **organisms** that are found everywhere on Earth, including the human gut.

The scars on the face of this Afghan boy, photographed in the 1970s, show that he has survived a smallpox infection. Smallpox was finally stamped out in 1980, but it could still be used as a biological weapon.

Deadly viruses

Viruses that may be used in **CBW** warfare include smallpox and **VHFs**. Smallpox was a deadly disease around the world until a global health campaign finally stamped it out in 1980. At least two laboratories, one in Russia and one in the USA, kept samples of smallpox for research. The US Center for Disease Control has about 500 different breeds of smallpox in a freezer, to help scientists create **vaccines** (medicines that stop viruses) in an emergency.

The initials VHF stand for Viral Haemorrhagic Fever. These viruses cause heavy bleeding and fevers, and often lead to death. The VHF family of viruses are very infectious. They include Ebola, Marburg and Hanta. All of them cause terrible internal bleeding, and even bleeding from skin pores and eyes. The natural version of the Ebola virus is widespread in Africa. It is often deadly, although it can be survived with proper medical care. However, a military version might be even more dangerous. It is not known if any country has succeeded in creating a VHF weapon.

Harmful bacteria

Very few bacteria are deadly to humans, but two types of bacteria that are used in research into bioweapons are anthrax and **botulinum**. Anthrax is the most famous bacteria in bioweapons research. Though harmful to cattle, it is not normally powerful enough to kill a fit human being, unless it is inhaled as a cloud of microscopic dust particles. Botulinum is not deadly in itself, but produces a poison called Botulinum **Toxin**, which is the most powerful **nerve agent** known to science. Other bacteria that have been used as weapons include bubonic plague, swine fever and glanders – a bacteria that is used to kill horses.

The highly dangerous Ebola virus is a type of VHF. It is seen here through a very powerful microscope.

CBWs on the battlefield

CBWs can be very hard to deliver to an enemy in large quantities. In practice, four methods of delivery have been used in battle. The first method involves waiting until the wind is blowing towards the enemy and then releasing CBW gases or dust into the air. But wind direction is hard to predict. If the wind changes, CBWs can be carried back to the troops that are using the weapons, and have terrible effects on them. The second method is to fly over enemy positions and drop breakable 'bottles' of CBW material. The third is to fire 'shells' filled with CBW material, which break open on impact. The fourth is to load the **agent** into a large spray tank – like a large-scale aerosol can – and fasten the can to the underside of a jet aircraft. In this way very large areas can be covered with the agent. The spray method was used to clear large areas of jungle, using chemical **defoliants**, during the Vietnam War.

In World War I, **mustard gas** was often carried towards enemy soldiers by the wind. In this photograph, US soldiers act out the horror of a gas attack, to prepare other soldiers for battle.

CBWs and the weather

The weather poses big challenges for CBW warfare. Biological weapons normally need a particular temperature and moisture to remain active – the wrong weather or even sunlight can kill the germs. However, testing of biological agents in a remote part of Scotland (Gruinard Island) showed that anthrax – one of the most effective and long-lasting biological warfare agents – can remain in a weakened form in the soil for a period of up to 50 years. Some chemical weapons stay active longer in cold weather, and this may make it dangerous to capture territory abandoned by an enemy after a successful chemical weapons attack.

Protection and transport

CBW warfare is not simply about having the technology to make a weapon. Military commanders have to be able to defend against CBW attacks as well. They need gadgets to check what is in the air, CBW-proof suits and gas masks to protect soldiers, airtight vehicles and buildings for the CBW victims, and medical support to treat casualties. Troops need to be well trained, and may be given drugs or **vaccines** to protect them against some CBWs. Each of these measures costs money and time, and the use of drugs and vaccines may expose troops to new dangers.

Weapons are normally made a long way from the battlefield and then shipped to it. For CBWs, special ships or planes may be needed to do this safely. If they are not dropped from planes as bombs, CBWs need to be stored where they can be reached if needed. As with all **ammunition** stores, this is dangerous – enemy fire could break open a store. In the case of CBWs, if the active agents are released in the wrong place, an army could be poisoned, or cut off from its supplies and its lines of retreat.

11

CBWs through the ages

Sometimes, harmless-looking plants can be used as deadly weapons. The ancient Greeks used the root of the hellebore plant to poison the water supplies of enemy cities.

The first well-documented example of **CBW** warfare appears in history books about World War I. But chemical and biological weapons were used much earlier than that. Some of the evidence is hard to be certain about, because people often used CBWs without any scientific understanding of how they worked.

Humans have known about **toxins** in nature for thousands of years. Some native people, such as the Wai-Wai of Guyana, in South America, still harvest poisonous plants and catch poisonous animals, so that they can use these toxins on arrows or darts when they are hunting animals. Poisons like these must have been used against other humans in early warfare.

The ancient Greeks used poisonous plants as chemical weapons. They put roots from the hellebore plant into the water supply of cities in order to force the defenders to abandon the city. They also burnt sulphur when the wind was blowing towards an enemy army. This created nasty, choking clouds and disabled the enemy troops.

Plague attack

The most famous early use of a biological weapon was in 1346. At this time a terrible disease – the bubonic plague, also known as the 'Black Death' – was spreading from China towards Europe, carried by merchants along the trading routes. When the plague reached present-day Ukraine, it infected an army of **Tartars** who were trying to reclaim the city of Kaffa from Italian traders. Instead of burying their dead, the Tartars threw the plague victims over the city walls, to infect the Italians. Some surviving traders managed to escape from the city, but they carried the deadly disease with them back to Italy. The Black Death was extremely infectious and spread amazingly quickly, killing almost a third of Europe's population within five years.

Spreading smallpox

Another cruel use of a biological weapon took place in Canada in 1763. British soldiers fighting the Native Americans smeared pus from smallpox victims on to blankets and then sent the blankets as a gift to their enemies. The disease spread very rapidly through the Native American people, and even succeeded in driving off George Washington's American army in 1766. British troops were given an early type of **vaccination** to protect them from this deadly 'weapon'.

This picture from a medieval manuscript shows people suffering from the Black Death. Some of the victims of the Black Death were used as deadly biological weapons in the siege of Kaffa.

World War I (1914–18)

During World War I, warfare changed dramatically. New technologies – submarines, tanks, machine guns, aircraft, high explosives and poison gases – all provided new ways to fight a war. Most importantly, nations at war began to think in terms of killing large numbers of the enemy at once.

At 5 p.m. on 22 April 1915, fighting at Ypres, Belgium, was drawing to an end for the day when troops fighting for the **Allies** noticed a weird, greenish cloud approaching them from the German **trenches**. They were seeing the first serious gas attack of the war. The chlorine gas blinded and choked the men who breathed it in. By 5:30 p.m., the Allies were forced to abandon a 3-kilometre (2-mile) stretch of their trenches. Unprotected German troops followed behind the cloud of gas, capturing several villages and big guns. It was a dramatic introduction to the power of chemical warfare. The Allied troops were shocked and frightened.

Several countries that were not involved in the war spoke out against this cruel use of gas. But by the end of the war, all sides would be using chlorine and other, more deadly gases. Soon, gas masks were invented to protect soldiers, as well as better ways to deliver the gas in shells, rather than just releasing it into the wind. But gas was not a reliable weapon, and its effects were so horrible that it was banned after the war. Roughly 100,000 soldiers were killed by gas in World War I and another 900,000 or so were badly injured, with permanently burnt and scarred lungs that made breathing difficult for the rest of their lives.

British soldiers, blinded by a **mustard gas** attack in 1918, form a line to follow a man who can see.

"Men marched asleep. Many had lost their boots,
But limped on, blood-shod. All went lame, all blind;
Drunk with fatigue; deaf even to the hoots
Of gas-shells dropping softly behind.

Gas! Gas! Quick, boys! An ecstasy of fumbling,
Fitting the clumsy helmets just in time,
But someone still was yelling out and stumbling
And floundering like a man in fire or lime.
Dim through the misty panes and thick green light,
As under a green sea, I saw him drowning.
In all my dreams, before my helpless sight,
He plunges at me, guttering, choking, drowning."

Lines describing a gas attack during the World War I, from the poem 'Dulce et Decorum est', by the British soldier and poet, Wilfred Owen.

World War II (1939–45)

In the years following World War I, scientists in many countries carried out research into new forms of poison gas. But during World War II, the threat of **retaliation** was enough to keep these new weapons in storage – neither side wanted to risk the possibility that the other might have a 'super-weapon'. Even so, thousands were injured or killed by chemical **agents**, when storage or transport tanks leaked, or broke open during bombing raids.

In 1943 a ship belonging to the **Allies**, the *John Harvey*, was blown open at Bari, Italy, killing 69 people and disabling hundreds. The ship had been carrying a top-secret shipment of **mustard gas** to the battlefront. The gas leaked, and all the officers who knew the secret were killed trying to stop the gas from spreading. This meant that no warning could be given to survivors on the ship, or to the people of Bari, or to any medical staff who could have treated them.

A London air raid warden fits a young boy with a gas mask in 1939, to protect him against possible gas attacks on the city. Gas masks like this, which were specially designed for children, were known as 'Mickey Mouse' masks.

The Holocaust

The most horrific use of chemicals ever known took place during World War II, when Hitler's Nazi party attempted to murder millions of Jewish citizens. This terrible massacre came to be known as the Holocaust. Jews and others – such as gypsies and the disabled – were rounded up into **concentration camps**, where the Nazis forced them into slave labour or gassed them to death.

Zyklon B was a German **pesticide** that was used to kill insects such as **lice**. It was based on prussic acid, which is a deadly poison. At first, the Nazis used Zyklon B to control lice among the prisoners, but then they began using it to gas Jewish people to death, hundreds at a time. By the end of World War II, roughly six million Jews had been killed. It is impossible to prove how many were gassed, and how many were shot, starved or worked to death. However, it is known that Zyklon B was used to kill over a million people at Auschwitz concentration camp in Poland.

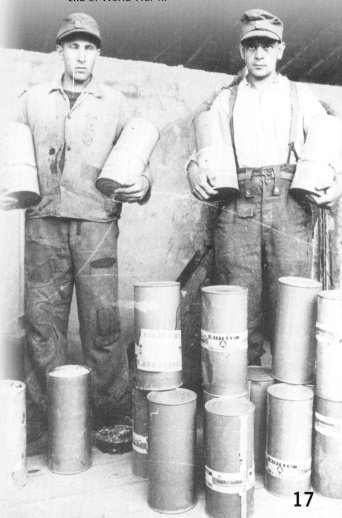

Soldiers from the **Soviet Union** display canisters of deadly Zyklon B, found in Auschwitz concentration camp at the end of World War II.

The Cold War (1945–90)

Two main powers emerged from World War II – the USA and the **Soviet Union** (USSR). Both countries had major **CBW** research programmes. At the end of World War II, the USA had gained new CBW expertise from Germany when German scientists fled to America, in order to avoid being captured by the Soviet troops who were marching through Germany. The USA also gained valuable information from the UK, as British scientists provided full details of their experiments into biological warfare.

The USA and the USSR had different ideas about how the post-war world should be run. They battled for control of the world, but never fought in open conflict against each other. Instead the two countries supported opposite sides in wars in other parts of the world. This period of hostility lasted from the end of World War II to the start of the 1990s and is called the **Cold War**. During the Cold War, neither side could be sure that the other would use CBWs, so both sides did research. They also shared some CBW knowledge and technology with the other countries that they supported.

While the USA and the USSR were carrying out this research, the British army had learnt to use weedkillers to make it easier to fight rebels in the jungles of Malaysia. They used powerful weedkillers to destroy large areas of jungle, exposing enemy soldiers to attacks from the air. US scientists learnt from the British and developed chemicals such as Agent Orange. This was a highly poisonous **defoliant** that was used to strip away vast areas of jungle during the war between US troops and **communist** rebels in Vietnam.

Problems and slowdown

In the USA, CBW research was carried out on volunteers at Camp Detrick (now Fort Detrick). The details of most of these tests are still classified (kept secret), but the US military claims that it gained useful new knowledge about defending soldiers from CBW attacks. At the same time, **delivery systems** for CBWs were tested at Dugway, Utah. In 1968, over 6000 sheep were killed near the base at Dugway, when a delivery system for the **nerve agent** VX jammed open on a test aircraft, causing a deadly cloud to drift for miles outside the target area. Then, in 1969, scientists found traces of a **bioweapon** in blood samples from wildlife living around Dugway and voters became much less tolerant of CBW research. President Nixon announced that the USA was stopping its research and development into biological warfare, and during the late 1960s and early 1970s the USA began to dismantle its **offensive** programme and started to destroy its CBWs.

In the late 1980s, the Soviet Union fell apart and the Cold War came to an end. This marked the end of one chapter in the history of CBW warfare.

The Iran-Iraq War (1980–88)

Towards the end of the **Cold War**, there was a major case of a country using **CBW**s in open warfare. This was the Iran-Iraq War, which lasted from 1980 to 1988. In 1979, a revolution in Iran put a strict Islamic leader into power. The countries of the West and the **Soviet Union** were both concerned about this new Islamic power in the region, so each in their own way helped Iraq to fight a war against Iran. Some of this help is on public record, such as 21 anthrax samples shipped to Iraq from Fort Detrick and a germ 'library' in Maryland. Iraq used CBWs in the war as early as 1983. In one battle in 1986, the Iraqis used **mustard gas** and the **nerve agent** tabun, killing up to 10,000 of the enemy.

Mustard gas and nerve gas were both used against Iran's foot soldiers. Iraq also used chemical bombs and **missiles** against Iranian war headquarters. At the very end of the war, there was a battle for control of the town of Halabja in northern Iraq. The town was held by rebel **Kurds**, who wanted to use the war to free their region from the control of the Iraqi government. Many thousands of rebel fighters and their families were poisoned in a massive Iraqi CBW attack.

Kurdish guerrillas inspect an unexploded chemical bomb, dropped by Iraqi planes on the rebel town of Halabja in 1988.

Some experts believe that this terrible event, together with Iraq's new long-range missiles, convinced the leaders of Iran that they should make peace with Iraq. The Iranians feared that Iraq was now capable of striking the Iranian capital city, Tehran, with chemical weapons. **Bioweapons** had been too difficult for Iraq to perfect, but research was well under way and the Iranians were afraid of what might happen in the future.

The technology that Iraq gained during the war was not forgotten afterwards. Top-secret research continued in Iraq after the war, leading the **UN** to become concerned that Iraq might use these weapons again, perhaps against Israel or even on its own citizens. In 1990, Iraq invaded its neighbour, Kuwait. UN forces drove Iraq out of Kuwait in 1991, and the UN demanded that Iraq destroy all its CBWs and end its CBW research. By 2002, the UN was still not sure that Iraq, led by Saddam Hussein, had given up CBWs. An American-led military force invaded Iraq in 2003 to **disarm** Saddam's **regime**.

Continued problems

By the end of the 20th century, it seemed that the threat of a large-scale war using **CBW**s was fading, but a new challenge had taken its place. The biggest impact of CBW warfare at the start of the 21st century was the huge task of clearing up the mess created in the previous century.

Cleaning up

With the growth of environmental awareness, it is now illegal to dump CBWs at sea, as happened after 1945. Also, the collapse of the **Soviet Union** has left Russia too poor to invest in safe disposal of CBW stockpiles. This leaves a massive task for other countries in the world. Some countries have built special factories to destroy CBWs, and a few – such as the USA, Germany and Sweden – have given Russia money to help it build its own disposal factories. The work of safe disposal will take several decades, and the risk of leaks and accidents will continue until all CBWs are destroyed.

Casualties of CBW

At the same time as countries are trying to destroy old CBWs, the world also has to handle the effects of previous CBW warfare on humans and their environment. The **defoliant** used in the Vietnam War, Agent Orange, has harmed or disabled as many as one million Vietnamese citizens, as well as US troops and their children. Agent Orange has been linked with a type of diabetes, disabilities in babies, cancers and miscarriages. Some governments now pay their war **veterans** extra money to help them meet the cost of these injuries.

Case study Dangerous bombs

CBWs from World War I still threaten northern Europe. Shells containing **mustard gas** and other poisons are often found by people, such as farmers and builders, who disturb the ground where battles were once fought. When the shells are discovered they must be taken to safe collection points. In 2001, the town of Vimy in France had to be **evacuated** when a collection point containing 173 tons of these 85-year-old bombs was found to be unsafe – some of the bombs had leaked. Fortunately, no one was harmed.

Still in use?

The use and development of chemical and biological weapons is not just a thing of the past. Around 65 countries have promised to destroy all their stocks over the next two decades, but many are still researching CBWs to keep their defence technology up to date. No large military power would be happy to end its CBW programme while the technology still exists in other parts of the world.

False alarms?

Countries that are involved in wars often make the claim that their enemy has used CBW warfare, in order to gain public sympathy. North Korea, Iraq and Cuba have each blamed the USA for outbreaks of crop-damaging insects in their countries. Good scientific proof has not been found for any of these cases, and very few people believe them to be true.

Leftover Agent Orange in Vietnam causes birth defects in thousands of children each year. These two Vietnamese boys are both victims of Agent Orange.

CBWs and terrorism

In the 21st century one of the greatest threats of **CBW** warfare may come from **terrorists**. After the **Cold War**, the number of terrorist attacks fell steadily, as many conflicts came to an end. However, in recent years, terror attacks have become more random (not directed at a specific enemy) and more deadly. In the past, terrorists had usually pinpointed 'enemy' soldiers or politicians, for example bombing army barracks where soldiers lived. But by 2001, their targets were often ordinary **civilians**. This change has made CBW warfare by terrorists a real risk – the danger to innocent lives appears to have become less of a concern to terrorists.

A terrorist weapon

The first major case of a random terrorist CBW attack happened in 1995, in Japan. There, the powerful religious **cult**, Aum Shinrikyo, used its wealth to make a **nerve agent** called sarin. Scientists working for the cult did secret tests on animals in Australia, before releasing the gas in Tokyo's metro system. Twelve people died and over 1000 were hospitalized as a result of the attack. By luck, the sarin gas made for this mission was weaker than anything the cult had made before – otherwise several thousands more people could have been killed.

Japanese workers remove drums full of **toxic** chemicals from the Aum Shinrikyo laboratory, following a police raid on the cult's headquarters.

An anti-terrorist weapon

In October 2002, 40 terrorists from Chechnya, a rebel province in southern Russia, held around 750 people hostage inside a theatre in the Russian city of Moscow. They demanded an end to Russia's military rule of Chechnya and threatened to kill all the hostages if the Russian government did not agree to their demands. After three days, Russian security forces stormed the theatre, using a knock-out gas to stop the terrorists killing everyone. The gas was very effective, but 129 hostages died from the side effects of the gas, when they were unable to breathe. The Russian government was criticized for using the gas, despite rescuing around 700 hostages. CBW warfare had changed once more – this time it was used in the battle to fight terrorism.

Russian Interior Ministry troops take up their positions outside the Moscow theatre, before storming the building using an anaesthetic gas.

What gas?

The Russian government's use of gas against the Chechen hostage-takers surprised the world. At first, no one knew what the gas might be, and this caused fear that medical staff would not be able to deal with casualties in the best way. But the Russian authorities told doctors to treat survivors as if they had taken too much of an opium-based drug, such as heroin. After several days, the Russian authorities said that they had used a type of anaesthetic – a gas used by doctors to send people to sleep when they are having operations. Because its security forces had used a medical gas, Russia had not broken any laws about researching or using chemical weapons.

Anthrax attacks

Following the **terrorist** attacks in New York and Washington, on 11 September 2001, there was a series of anthrax attacks in the USA. In late September, someone mailed anthrax to journalists and politicians. The first two letters contained anthrax particles that were too small to float free of the paper and infect many people. But two more letters contained particles that formed a dust cloud that could be inhaled. In total, five people died, including two postal workers. As a precaution, roughly 30,000 people at high risk were treated with **antibiotics** to protect them against the deadly effects of anthrax.

Anthrax research

The anthrax attacks in the US postal system alerted the public to the danger of **CBW**s. If the anthrax attacker had used better technology, thousands or even millions of people might have been infected. Stocks of antibiotics would have run out, and tens of thousands could have died. The FBI (the USA's special police force) studied the risks from anthrax attackers and considered a range of possible **delivery systems**. One possible delivery system investigated by the FBI was crop-spraying aircraft – these planes have spray tanks that could be filled with anthrax. In September 2001, the USA's 3000 crop-sprayers were not allowed to fly, while the FBI carried out their investigation.

In the months following the terrorist attacks on the USA in September 2001, some people feared that crop-spraying planes could be used to spread anthrax.

Fortunately, US security forces were soon able to calm some of the public's fears. The FBI found that anthrax could be grown using normal industrial equipment. However, there were three major reasons why a full-scale anthrax attack would be less likely than had been feared. First, the basic equipment needed would cost about US $1 million and was not freely available in most countries. Second, terrorists would need a special breed of anthrax – a type that is only found in top-security military research labs. Third, only a few military scientists around the world knew how to process anthrax into its most dangerous,

dust form. Even the wealthy and highly skilled Japanese Aum Shinrikyo **cult** (see page 24) had failed to make it.

It was also found that crop-sprayers were not as risky as feared. Pilots need extreme skill to fly them, especially when loaded. They would also need some very complicated changes to be able to spray a fine cloud of anthrax dust. Sprayed as a liquid, anthrax would be relatively harmless to humans, although it might harm farm animals grazing on **contaminated** grass.

Real and imagined fears

Chemical and biological warfare appeals to **terrorists** not just because of its destructive potential, but also because even the idea of these weapons causes fear. The difficult science of **CBW**s leaves most people unable to make sense of the risks for themselves. This public fear may become more damaging to a country than an actual attack. In order to show that they are protecting their country, politicians may have to make extra laws, and find money for a wide range of security measures. The security measures may cause delay, inconvenience and even new risks.

Across the world, in the weeks following the attacks of 11 September 2001, hundreds of businesses, transport systems and schools had their usual schedules interrupted by anthrax hoaxes and false alarms. Buildings were sealed for hours before people could return to work. Airports and railway stations had to be closed. It has not been possible to add up all the hours of useful activity that were lost around the world as a result of these scares.

Emergency service workers in New York practise how to deal with a nerve agent attack. Rehearsals like this are very important, but they can also cause alarm.

Sterilizing mail

In the USA, every piece of mail sent to government offices now has to pass through a machine that **sterilizes** it. Any **bacteria** in the mail is destroyed by this machine. However, there is some evidence that this 'clean' mail is riskier for postal workers to handle than normal mail – the process dries out the paper, making it dustier and more likely to irritate the skin and lungs. In addition, the extra step in the process of mail delivery adds time and cost to postal services.

> **"**Had we not hit that target [the Al Shifa factory] and had bin Laden used chemical weapons in a terrorist attack, I don't know how we could have looked the American people in the face.**"**
>
> Sandy Berger, US National Security Adviser, justifying the US attack on the Al Shifa factory in 1998

Workers inspect the ruins of the Al Shifa medicine factory, which was destroyed by US missiles in the mistaken belief that it was a chemical weapons factory.

Dual-use items

There are other sorts of costs created by combatting CBW terrorism. CBW makers often use equipment and materials that have a **dual use** – a military one and an innocent **civilian** use, such as making medicines. Controlling dual-use items can help to prevent the creation of deadly CBWs, but can also delay progress on vital social and medical projects. In one case, concern over dual-use led to disaster. In 1998, the USA launched a **missile** attack on the Al Shifa medicine factory in Khartoum (East Africa) because it feared that the factory was manufacturing CBWs. The attack was meant to prevent a CBW terror campaign against the USA. However, CBWs were not being manufactured there, and the attack knocked out one of East Africa's best resources in the life-or-death struggle against malaria and other diseases.

Are CBWs worse than other weapons?

CBW warfare is usually thought to be worse than other types of warfare. However, it is not always easy to understand why this is the case. All kinds of warfare cause terrible suffering and death, so why are CBWs considered to be so much worse?

Killing civilians

One argument against CBW warfare is that **civilians** should not be killed in war. CBWs will kill or injure anyone – soldier, civilian or child – who is exposed to them. However, almost every war in the last 150 years has involved civilians, either killing them or destroying their lives in other ways.

Since the end of World War II, nations have tried to avoid killing civilians in warfare. But this is almost impossible to avoid in industrial societies with large cities. If CBW warfare is opposed in order to prevent the large-scale killing of innocent civilians, it could be argued that there should also be a ban on the use of high-flying aircraft to drop bombs on cities, as these also cause countless civilian deaths.

Excessive force

Many people would agree that it is morally acceptable for individuals to use force to defend themselves against an attack. But this self-defence should not involve the use of unnecessary force. For example, it is not usually right to respond to being punched by using a knife or a gun. This idea can be applied to large-scale warfare, as well. It can be argued that the disabilities suffered by people in a CBW attack are much worse than the usual injuries that soldiers might expect to risk in battle. However, this argument against the use of CBWs needs to be balanced against the effects of other types of weapon, such as **fuel-air explosives**, which also cause terrible lung damage.

A different attitude

Most people find the use of CBWs unacceptable because it reflects a particularly uncaring attitude to the victims of an attack. While it is possible to argue that the use of **conventional weapons** shows some respect for the enemy soldiers' ability to fight back, users of CBWs are treating their victims as if they were less than human. The Nazis' use of poison gas in the **concentration camps** is especially shocking because the prisoners were not treated like human beings, but like fleas or **lice** that had to be destroyed.

Causing disease

Throughout human history people have made enormous efforts to fight disease and heal the sick. In all cultures, healing and caring for the sick are seen to be very important human virtues. Because of these attitudes to disease, using a weapon that deliberately causes disease and sickness seems especially wrong.

CBWs are not the only weapons that cause large-scale destruction. This photograph shows part of London, UK, which was badly damaged by bombs during World War II.

Is CBW research justified?

Scientific knowledge cannot just be forgotten, and people today have to live with the fact of **CBW** warfare. It is every country's right to defend itself, and countries expect to test and improve their defences against a possible CBW attack.

Defence or attack?

Most industrialized countries have chemical and biological defence programmes. The role of these programmes is to evaluate the threat that is posed by CBWs and prepare the country's defences against their possible use. Research into defences against chemical or biological warfare is allowed under both the Chemical Weapons Convention (or **CWC**) and the Biological Weapons Convention (or **BWC**) set up by the **UN** (see page 35).

To prepare to defend their country against a CBW attack, scientists have to learn a great deal about how CBWs work. However, this research may open up possibilities for the development of new kinds of chemical or biological weapon. A scientist who is working to help the country's security will be creating knowledge that could be turned to making weapons. If a politician decides to turn that knowledge to bad ends, some say it is unfair to blame the scientists.

Part of the job of CBW research scientists is to discover antidotes – medicines that can overcome the effects of CBWs. This is obviously valuable work. However, some people argue that scientists should refuse any CBW research job. But most of us would want to take medicines discovered by CBW researchers if there were a CBW attack.

CBW research involves testing protective clothing. This man is wearing an NBC suit (nuclear, biological and chemical). His hand is out to stop people entering a contaminated area.

This painting shows a child being **vaccinated** against smallpox in the 1820s. Today, researchers work on new antidotes and vaccines, and governments keep supplies of smallpox vaccine ready for use in case of a biological attack.

A dangerous business

Apart from the questions about whether CBW research is right or wrong, the fact that scientists need to work on CBWs in order to do their research creates great risks. The anthrax used in September and October 2001 appears to have been stolen from a US research lab. Some people argue that the risk of such thefts outweighs the benefits of better defence and medical knowledge.

CBW research has sometimes caused human casualties. The centre of British CBW research between 1939 and 1989 was a site called Porton Down in southern England. The programme there exposed roughly 20,000 'volunteers' to chemical weapons. At the time, many thought they were there to help scientists discover a cure for the common cold, but in fact they were being used for experiments with **nerve agents**. At least one soldier was accidentally killed during nerve gas experiments in 1953 at Porton Down, and others have since claimed to have suffered long-term health effects. However, there has been no hard evidence of this.

Subjects of similar nerve gas experiments in Canada and Australia, who suffered burns and blisters, have recently been awarded **compensation**.

Treaties and agreements

The United Nations plays a vital role in controlling the use of chemical and biological weapons around the world. This photograph shows members of the UN Security Council voting to approve CBW inspections in Iraq, in 2002.

Like any society, a community of nations tries to agree and live by laws that are in the best interests of everyone. These international laws have a range of names such as treaty, convention and protocol. They are all contracts signed by politicians on behalf of the nations they represent.

Early agreements

The first known **CBW** warfare treaty was signed between the French and Germans in Strasbourg in 1675. The two nations agreed not to use poisoned bullets in any future war between them.

Two treaties banning the use of poisonous gas were signed in 1874 and 1899 by several powerful nations. But there was very little chance of being found guilty and punished under these laws, because there was no world 'police force'. Another effort was made in 1925 to create rules that would work better. The Geneva Protocol banned countries from being the first to use CBWs, but not from researching or stockpiling them. It also allowed the nations that had signed the Geneva Protocol to use CBWs against those who had not signed – which included most of the less developed world.

The Geneva Protocol managed to prevent the use of CBWs in World War II. Because it gave nations the right to strike back against a CBW attack, no country was ready to make the first move and risk this result. But it did nothing to stop CBW research.

Two conventions

By the 1970s, CBW technology was becoming harder to keep secret. In 1972, the Biological Weapons Convention (**BWC**) was agreed by leading countries at the **UN** and it came into force in 1975. The BWC outlaws biological weapons, and asks all nations to destroy their stocks and end research into **offensive** weapons. A total of 147 countries have signed up to this treaty.

The Chemical Weapons Convention (**CWC**) was first created in 1993 and came into force in April 1997. By 2003, a total of 151 countries had signed up to the treaty. The CWC sets out tougher rules than the BWC, and provides a timetable for destroying chemical weapons.

The Australia Group

Side by side with these international agreements, countries work together in other ways to control CBW warfare. The Australia Group is a club of the world's leading countries, formed to keep an eye on possibly dangerous technology and materials. Together, they agree on measures to control the export of certain chemicals, biological **agents** and **dual-use** materials and technology, so that exports of these items from their countries do not contribute to the increase of CBWs.

During the 1970s, US President Richard Nixon called a halt to most of his country's bioweapons research, inspiring other UN countries to do the same.

Policing the laws

United Nations' weapons inspectors are viewed through a gateway as they examine a **missile** factory in Iraq in January 2003.

"It is simply impractical to declare all potential dual-capable facilities, as these would encompass beer brewers, yogurt makers and many academic laboratories."

Dr Edward Lacey, US State Department, on possible changes to the BWC

The Biological Weapons Convention (**BWC**) has no police force to back it up. Countries are relied on to follow the rules as agreed, and to police each other. If one country has reason to suspect another of a secret **bioweapons** programme, it is up to the countries involved to work out an agreement between themselves or to go to the **UN** to ask for inspections to be arranged.

The Chemical Weapons Convention (**CWC**) is generally thought to have a stronger set of rules than the BWC. It has set up a policing group, the Organization for the Prohibition of Chemical Weapons (**OPCW**), which can launch surprise visits on suspected weapons sites in almost every country in the world.

Site inspections

Site inspections are the best way to prove – or disprove – complaints about a nation's **CBW** programme. But it is hard to force a country to agree to an inspection against its will. Countries can and do resist inspections, arguing that their security may be weakened. There can be several reasons for a country wanting to resist inspections. For example, the country being inspected may suspect the inspectors of spying, or of stealing CBW secrets to help their own countries' programmes. However, measures are in place to make sure that neither national security nor trade secrets are put at risk by inspections.

Dual-use checks

Dual-use technology is the toughest nut to crack. The same factory and almost the same materials can be used one week to produce chemical weapons, and the next to make farm fertilizers. Inspection teams have to rely on good information and a keen eye for detail, such as unusual safety precautions, in order to discover whether a factory is really manufacturing chemical weapons. This makes the weapons inspectors' job very difficult, and it is possible to make bad mistakes. The Al Shifa medicines factory in East Africa which was bombed by mistake in 1998 (see page 29) was found, after it had been destroyed, to have no airlocks or sealed rooms – both vital precautions for working with CBW materials.

Punishing the lawbreakers

All the efforts of the organizations for the prohibition of **CBW**s would be pointless if the international community, represented by the **UN**, could not enforce the organizations' decisions. Agreements on the use of CBWs which have failed in the past have done so mainly because they were seen to lack 'bite' and to be impossible to enforce. A country that is caught pursuing CBW projects has to be persuaded or forced to change its mind. This poses a problem for the UN. On the one hand, it must decide what type of response or punishment is correct. On the other hand, it has to think about the likely bad effects of the UN response on ordinary **civilians** in the country.

Different responses

In the best case, a country's government may be persuaded by careful discussion or negotiation. This approach is called diplomacy and it provides the least harmful solution. The next level of response is to break off diplomatic relations. This makes the country very isolated. It may also mean that the country misses out on taking part in international decisions on other issues that are important to its future.

A third level of response is for some countries to stop trading with a country. This is known as boycotting or using sanctions. This response damages the country's economy, but is likely to harm poor people more than the powerful. It also only works with small economies – few poor countries could afford to boycott rich ones.

The last level is military response. This might simply mean putting armed forces in position to attack. It might also mean bombing a few targets, or it could mean a full-scale war. The military response will result in lives being lost and serious damage to property. The UN needs to have tried all other options before taking actions as serious as this. If CBW laboratories are attacked, they may release poisons into the environment, and this is the opposite of what the **CWC** and **BWC** conventions aim to achieve. The outcome of any military activity is hard to predict.

Military action is the final resort to prevent a government from using chemical or biological weapons. However, war can have terrible consequences for the ordinary people living in the country under attack.

Preparing for the worst

As well as signing up to international agreements to combat **CBW**s, governments also work at home to be prepared to deal with CBW warfare. A major part of this work is researching appropriate medical responses to an attack. In the event of a CBW attack, a government needs to be able to do several things quite quickly. It must find out which CBW has been used, select the best treatment for the victims of the attack, maintain the safety of health workers and make sure that it has enough medical resources to cope with the problem.

Japanese researchers have recently developed a new type of mask to help protect children from chemical and biological attacks.

Protective measures

CBW research scientists have created new **vaccines** and other medicines to protect people from the effects of CBW warfare. These medicines are kept in storage and soldiers and other people at risk may be given them as a precaution, before a CBW attack.

Scientists have developed special equipment to deal with CBW attacks. Armed forces now carry detector equipment that quickly warns soldiers about a CBW attack. Soldiers in danger areas are also issued with **NBC suits** ('nuclear, biological and chemical' suits) to protect them. The US President is followed everywhere by a security team with an NBC suit for him to wear in an emergency.

Safety suits protect soldiers during CBW warfare, but they are very hot to wear. Further testing and training is needed to help soldiers prepare for the extra stresses they will experience in battle when wearing this clothing. Other equipment tested in CBW research programmes includes armoured vehicles that are CBW-proof.

Coping with a CBW attack

Organizations such as the Red Cross are now able to offer **civilians** detailed advice about how to plan for an emergency and what they can do to help themselves survive CBW attacks. There are also kits available for use in emergencies, containing basic food and first-aid supplies for families.

As well as developing medicines to fight the effects of CBWs, researchers have also studied ways of coping with casualties who may be 'poisonous' to work with. Scientists are able to give medical staff special training for emergencies. With this knowledge, medical staff can avoid being injured or infected by any leftover CBW on their patients. They can also stop hospitals and ambulances being **contaminated** while caring for CBW casualties.

Specialized equipment has been developed to deal with CBW attacks. Here, an emergency worker is helped into a protective suit during an anthrax scare in South Africa, in October 2001.

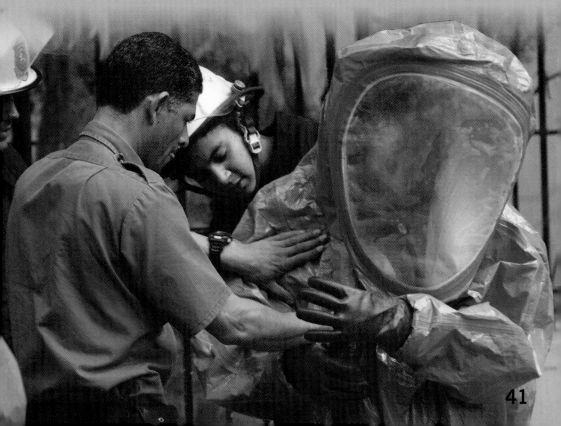

Emergency planning

Military planners use 'war games' and exercises to help them discover if their plans will work smoothly. But planning for an attack against **civilians** is a different matter. It is not possible to involve an entire population in a rehearsal. Instead, exercises are invented by experts to test how decision-makers would respond to a crisis.

Case study Dark Winter

In June 2001, experienced US leaders took part in a role-playing exercise. The game was intended to help them think about how they would cope in an emergency caused by a **CBW** attack. It was held around a conference table and lasted for a weekend. The game was called Dark Winter.

In the game, the US leaders pretended that they were all members of a National Security Council (NSC) – an organization that was responsible for making all the important decisions in time of war. The NSC faced a military problem on the Iraq/Kuwait border in the Persian Gulf, but at the first meeting the alarm was raised about a problem much closer to home. There was an outbreak of smallpox in the state of Oklahoma, with 20 known cases of the disease. The NSC agreed to keep some **vaccine** to be used to protect the army, in case this outbreak was caused by some form of CBW attack and the army was needed to help prevent it from spreading. Remaining stocks of vaccine were sent to affected areas, to try to stop the smallpox **virus** from spreading.

By week two in the exercise, 2000 Americans were infected, across fifteen states. The disease was widespread, and vaccine supplies were running out. The President addressed the nation to appeal for calm, but there was panic. People left the cities, carrying the disease with them. Hospitals were flooded with panicking people and casualties, and hospital staff were beginning to leave. Medical services were breaking down.

Soldiers can train to be prepared for a CBW attack. These Russian soldiers are carrying out an exercise in a special training centre for CBW protection.

❝If you're going against someone who is using a tool that you're not used to having him use – disease – and using it quite rationally and craftily toward an entirely unreasonable and god-awful end – we are in a world we haven't ever really been in before.❞

R. James Woolsey, former director of the CIA [Central Intelligence Agency] and participant in Dark Winter

Meanwhile, the military crisis in the Persian Gulf was hotting up. Could the USA afford to send more troops abroad?

By week three in the exercise, the US public was asking for the army to take over and contain the smallpox outbreak, but most of the army was in the Gulf. It was already beyond the power of the police or the national guards to trace and isolate all the infected people. By now 30,000 were infected, 1000 were dead, and the experts advised that, in the worst case, another million or so would die before new supplies of vaccine could be delivered. Then a letter from the smallpox **terrorists** arrived, admitting that they had started the outbreak and demanding that the USA pull all forces out of the Gulf, with a threat of further CBW attacks on the USA if they did not. The NSC was in a terrible position.

Dark Winter had revealed a big hole in the USA's CBW defences.

Non-governmental effort

Some organizations concerned with **CBW** warfare are not part of government. They are made up of experts and scientists or members of the public, who try to help reduce the risks of CBWs.

Anti-war protestors gather in Canada. Often, campaigns against CBWs are carried out 'behind the scenes'.

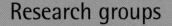

Research groups

Some groups of experts and scientists work on producing medicines and treatments to be used if a CBW attack takes place. For example, scientists do research to produce **antibiotics** and **vaccines** that will protect people against CBWs. Other experts develop technologies to give early warning that a CBW attack has taken place so that protective measures can be put into action. Experts and scientists also work on providing emergency management and response plans to reduce the risk posed by attacks.

Other kinds of expert work on chemical and biological warfare issues. These include historians, political scientists and experts in international law. Historians see how lessons from history may show us what might happen if we do not work to prevent the development of CBWs, and historians, political scientists and international lawyers look at how international agreements between countries can be strengthened in order to prevent chemical and biological warfare. Experts and scientists also help members of the public and campaigning organizations who are working to put an end to chemical and biological weapons.

Campaign groups

Campaign groups aim to bring CBW issues to the top of the heap of issues facing our politicians. They hope to make the problem of CBWs a priority for as many politicians as possible. **Lobby groups** do this quietly by approaching politicians directly, and providing them with useful facts and arguments. Other campaign groups tend to make more noise, trying to raise awareness in the media and among voters, so that the public make demands of their politicians, especially at election time. Both types of work need skill and determination to succeed – there are a lot of other issues that compete for public attention.

A few campaign groups take direct action to make their point. At this extreme, they may even break laws to publicize the dangers of chemical and biological weapons. For example, they might trespass on a military base to draw attention to secret CBW resources. Members of these groups believe that it is people's moral duty to fight against the use of CBWs, even if this means acting illegally. This sort of campaign is known as civil disobedience.

45

What are the risks?

People who are most at risk from **CBWs** can be given **vaccines** to help protect them. Here, British soldiers wait to be vaccinated at the start of the 1991 Gulf War.

Most of the information about **CBW** warfare is quite frightening, especially after the **terrorist** attacks on the USA in 2001. It can be very hard to make sense of the size of the risk when you read a newspaper headline about 'killer germs' on the loose. In 2001, some people were so sure that CBW terrorism was about to happen that they bought medical kits and gas masks for their families. Despite massive media coverage, millions of people did not understand how relatively small the risk posed by anthrax was. But it is easy to be misled about how risky something is.

Asking questions

Before taking action, claims about risks have to be carefully considered. People should ask a series of questions to get at the truth. Who is making the claim? Do they have a rounded view of all the issues? Do other experts agree with the claim? Is there good, solid research to back up the claim? Are the numbers used vague estimates or solid facts?

CBW warfare poses serious risks if a person has been exposed to CBW material. For example, smallpox kills roughly one in every three infected persons. But it is not correct to calculate from these figures that if there were a smallpox outbreak, one in every three people in a country would die. Not everyone would be infected with the disease and the quality of medical attention that people received, both in protecting and treating them, could have a big effect on how the disease affected them.

When journalists describe risks, they often focus on the worst case possible, since it tends to be more interesting. How many times have you heard a newsflash saying that something is actually pretty safe?

The risk to you from CBW warfare, unless you work in a military research programme, is too small to calculate with any accuracy. You can see some figures for comparative risks on page 50, which show just how small the risk is. Your chance of being killed by CBWs is very much less than your chance of being struck by lightning.

Some US families spent up to US$2000 on plastic 'bio-shelters' after reading frightening stories about terrorist attacks.

What can you do?

You might feel that your interest in chemistry or biology could be put to use in helping your country's national security. You might want to try to put an end to **CBW** warfare. Or you might think that this issue is not important enough to be worked up about it either way.

You and your friends could conduct a survey of public awareness of CBWs. It could be the starting point for some interesting debates.

Each of these viewpoints has good arguments for and against. The first thing you can do is to explore some of the Internet links at the back of this book, to find out more about the subject.

Raising awareness

Awareness of the issue is a good first step, and you might want to check how aware your friends and family are about CBWs. You could just ask them, or you could write out some questions and conduct a survey. Do people know the difference between chemical and biological weapons? Do they know what is allowed by international law and what is forbidden? Do they know which countries have CBW programmes? Do they know if their local politician is for or against CBW defence spending? When you have finished, see if you can see any pattern in the responses to your questions. You could also try organizing a debate on CBWs at your school or college.

If you want to make some people think further about the topic, try writing letters to your local politician. Be patient waiting for a reply. You will normally get a personal response within a month or two. You might want to take it further by writing to a newspaper or emailing a broadcaster when the issue comes up. Why not write to your local fire and health services, to ask what plans they have to cope with a CBW emergency?

Have a look at some of the campaign and **lobby groups** listed in the back of the book. Do any of them seem to be doing work that you think deserves some support?

> **"**I know not with what weapons World War III will be fought, but World War IV will be fought with sticks and stones.**"**
>
> The scientist, Albert Einstein, predicting that the weapons used in World War III would be so powerfully destructive that humanity would be reduced to living like primitive people once again

Facts and figures

Counting the human cost

These statistics show the numbers of deaths caused by different types of weapon:

Period	Type of weapon	Numbers killed
1945–92	conventional weapons	23,000,000
1945–92	nuclear weapons	400,000 (estimated total of cancer deaths due to nuclear tests)
1945–92	CBW weapons	approx. 100,000

Causes of death

This table lists causes of death in the USA. It shows how extremely small the risk of dying from CBW warfare is:

Heart disease	1 in 385
Accident	1 in 2928
Homicide (murder)	1 in 14,857
Electrocution	1 in 496,000
Commercial flight accident	1 in 1,568,000
Lightning	1 in 4,288,000
CBW warfare	less than all of the above

Chemical weapons controls

Countries that have declared a weapons programme to the Organization for the Prohibition of Chemical Weapons **(OPCW):**

USA

Russia

Countries that have refused the invitation to sign the Chemical Weapons Convention **(CWC):**

North Korea   Egypt

Iraq   Libya

Somalia   Syria

Chemical weapons or chemical weapons factories in the USA awaiting destruction

Chemical weapons:

Anniston Army Depot, Alabama; Redstone Arsenal, Alabama; Fort Richardson, Alaska; Pueblo Depot, Colorado; Johnston Atoll, Pacific Ocean; Blue Grass Army Depot, Kentucky; Unatiall Depot, Oregon; Camp Bullis, Texas; Dugway, Proving Ground, Utah; Tooele Army Depot, Utah

Chemical weapons factories:

Pine Bluff Arsenal, Arkansas; Rocky Mountain Arsenal, Colorado; Newport Chemical, Indiana; Aberdeen Proving Ground, Maryland

Countries that have not yet signed the Biological Weapons Convention (BWC)

(NB In many cases, the countries are simply too small to have a **bioweapons** programme)

Andorra	Marshall Islands
Angola	Mauritania
Antigua and Barbuda	Micronesia (Federal States of)
Azerbaijan	Moldova (Republic of)
Cameroon	Mozambique
Chad	Namibia
Comoros	Nauru
Cook Islands	Niue
Djibouti	Palau
East Timor	Samoa, Western
Eritrea	Sudan
Guinea	Tajikistan
Israel	Trinidad and Tobago
Kazakstan	Tuvalu
Kiribati	Zambia
Kyrgyzstan	

Further information

International contacts

The Australia Group
A non-proliferation organization representing most nations
www.australiagroup.net/index_en.htm

Organization for the Prohibition of Chemical Weapons
Johan de Wittlaan 32, 2517 JR,
The Hague, Netherlands
Tel: +31 (70) 416-3300
www.opcw.org
(Warning: history pages carry some disturbing pictures.)

Stockholm International Peace Research Institute
Signalistgatan 9, SE-169 70 Solna, Sweden
Tel: +46-8-655 97 00
http://projects.sipri.se/cbw/cbw-mainpage.html
Chemical and biological warfare pages
http://cbw.sipri.se/index2.html
A junior educational tour of SIPRI

The Transnational Foundation for Peace and Future Research
Vegagatan 25, S-224 57 Lund, Sweden
Tel: +46-46-145909
email: comments@transnational.org
www.transnational.org
An international network of peace organizations

Contacts in the UK

The Biological Weapons Convention
www.opbw.org
This website is maintained by the University of Bradford's Department of Peace Studies.

Jane's Defence Weekly
Sentinel House, 163 Brighton Road,
Coulsdon, Surrey CR5 2YH
Tel: 020 8700 3700
email: info@janes.co.uk
http://chembio.janes.com/
A site on CBWs

Contacts in the USA

Center for Civilian Biodefense Strategies
Tel: +1 (410) 223-1667
www.hopkins-biodefense.org

Centers for Disease Control and Prevention
1600 Clifton Road, Atlanta, GA 30333
www.bt.cdc.gov
US government bioterror information site

Center for Nonproliferation Studies
460 Pierce Street, Monterey, CA 93940
Tel: +1 (831) 647-4154
email: cns@miis.edu
http://cns.miis.edu/research/cbw

Chemical Weapons Convention
US Department of Commerce,
Bureau of Industry and Security,
Treaty Compliance Division,
1555 Wilson Boulevard, Suite 710,
Arlington, VA 22209-2405
www.cwc.gov

Council for a Livable World
110 Maryland Avenue NE,
Washington DC 20002
Tel: +1 (202) 543-4100
www.clw.org/involved.html
A US campaigning and **lobby group**

Federation of American Scientists
1717 K St. NW, Suite 209,
Washington DC 20036
Tel: +1 (202) 546-3300
www.fas.org/bwc/

The Nuclear Age Peace Foundation
PMB 121, 1187 Coast Village Road, Suite 1,
Santa Barbara, CA 93108-2794
Tel: +1 (805) 965-3443
email: youth@napf.org
www.wagingpeace.org

Public Broadcasting Service
www.pbs.org/wgbh/pages/frontline/shows/
plague
A feature on CBW warfare

Other Internet contacts

www.anthraxinvestigation.com/clueless.
html
An amateur detective examines an
anthrax panic

www.firstworldwar.com
Archive of information about World War 1

www.nizkor.org
Information on the Holocaust

www.redcross.org/pubs/dspubs/terrormat.
html
Advice from the American Red Cross on what
to do in the home to prepare for CBW warfare

Further reading

Chemical and Biological Warfare,
L B Taylor (Franklin Watts, 1992)

Understanding Germ Warfare (Science
Made Accessible), Sandy Fritz (Warner
Books, 2002)

Biological and Chemical Weapons (At
Issue), David M Haugen (Greenhaven
Press, 2001)

*Chemical and Biological Weapons in Our
Times*, Herbert M Levine (Franklin Watts,
2000)

*Chemical and Biological Warfare: The
Cruellest Weapons* (Issues in Focus),
Laurence P Pringle (Enslow Publishers,
2000)

Glossary

agent
something that has an effect

Allies
team formed by the UK, the USA and other countries to fight together on one side in World War I and World War II

ammunition
items such as bullets and shells, without which weapons such as guns or tanks are useless

antibiotic
medicine that kills bacteria. Different antibiotics affect different types of bacteria.

bacteria
single-celled organisms that live in all Earth environments, some of which benefit or harm other life forms

bioweapon
weapon that uses life forms to attack an enemy, or the enemy's support systems (such as animals or food crops). Bioweapon is short for biological weapons.

botulinum
poison-producing bacteria

BWC
international agreement made to outlaw biological weapons. The initials stand for Biological Weapons Convention.

CBW
initials standing for Chemical and Biological Weapons. The term CBW is used when talking about both types of weapon at once.

cell
basic, microscopic part of a living thing

civilian
any person who does not work for the military or security services of a country

Cold War
struggle for power between the USA and the Soviet Union, which was at its height in the 1950s and 1960s

communism
form of government where the state owns all the land and factories and provides for people's needs

compensation
money paid to someone to make up for harm that has been done to them

concentration camp
prison camp for civilians who are identified as possible enemies of the state, usually due to their ethnic group

contaminated
affected by something dirty or poisonous, such as a CBW. A contaminated object or substance can be very dangerous.

conventional weapons
weapons that are not nuclear, chemical or biological

cult
religious group that controls all aspects of its members' lives

CWC
international agreement made to outlaw chemical weapons. The initials stand for the Chemical Weapons Convention.

defoliant
chemical that makes leaves fall off plants and trees

delivery system
general term for the equipment used to deliver CBW materials to the enemy

disarm
to remove weapons or ammunition

dual-use
something that has two uses, for example, machinery or chemical substances that can be used for making CBWs, or for other purposes such as medicine or agriculture

evacuate
to move away from an area because it is dangerous

fuel-air explosive
large canister containing fuels that explode causing widespread damage

guerrilla
small group of troops that relies on surprise attacks and rapid escape before a larger force can respond

Kurds
people living mainly in northern Iraq, western Iran and eastern Turkey. Many Kurds in Iraq are fighting for their independence and freedom.

lice
small insects without wings that live on animals or people

lobby group
small political group that campaigns by talking directly to elected politicians

missile
weapon delivered to a target on a self-propelled rocket

mustard gas
chemical weapon that attacks the lungs and makes the skin blister

NBC suit
all-in-one suit including a gas mask, designed to protect its wearer from nuclear, biological and chemical warfare. The initials NBC stand for 'nuclear, biological and chemical'.

nerve agent
chemical that disables parts of the nervous system, such as the brain. Another name for nerve agent is nerve gas.

nuclear weapon
bomb or missile that turns matter into energy to cause a huge explosion

offensive
used for attacking

OPCW
policing group of the CWC. The initials stand for Organization for the Prohibition of Chemical Weapons.

organism
general term for any life form

pesticide
chemical designed to kill pests, usually insects

regime
system of government

retaliation
response to an attack with something just as deadly

Soviet Union
communist country made up of Russia and its neighbours, formed in 1922

sterilize
to make an object free of bacteria and viruses using X-rays, boiling water or chemicals, such as bleach

Tartars
warlike people from central Asia, sometimes also known as Mongols

terrorist
someone using violence or fear of violence to achieve political aims

toxin
poison

trench
deep ditch dug along the front lines on a battlefield, where soldiers can hide from the enemy's bullets

UN
international body set up in 1945 to promote international peace and cooperation. The initials stand for 'United Nations'.

vaccine
harmless version of a disease that 'teaches' the body to defend itself against that disease. Vaccines are given in a type of injection called a vaccination.

veteran
soldier or ex-soldier who has been involved in a war

VHF
initials standing for 'Viral Haemorrhagic Fever'. VHFs are viruses that cause heavy bleeding and fevers, and often lead to death.

virus
organism that reproduces by 'stealing' resources from the cells of other organisms. Many viruses cause diseases.

Index

Titles in the *Just the Facts* series include:

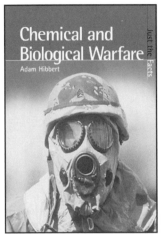

Hardback   0 431 16160 7

Hardback   0 431 16161 5

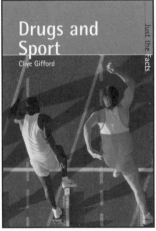

Hardback   0 431 16162 3

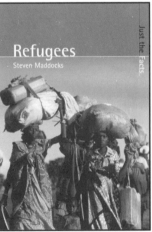

Hardback   0 431 16163 1

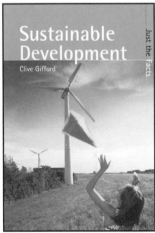

Hardback   0 431 16164 X

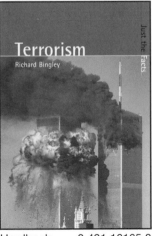

Hardback   0 431 16165 8

Find out about the other titles in this series on our website www.heinemann.co.uk/library